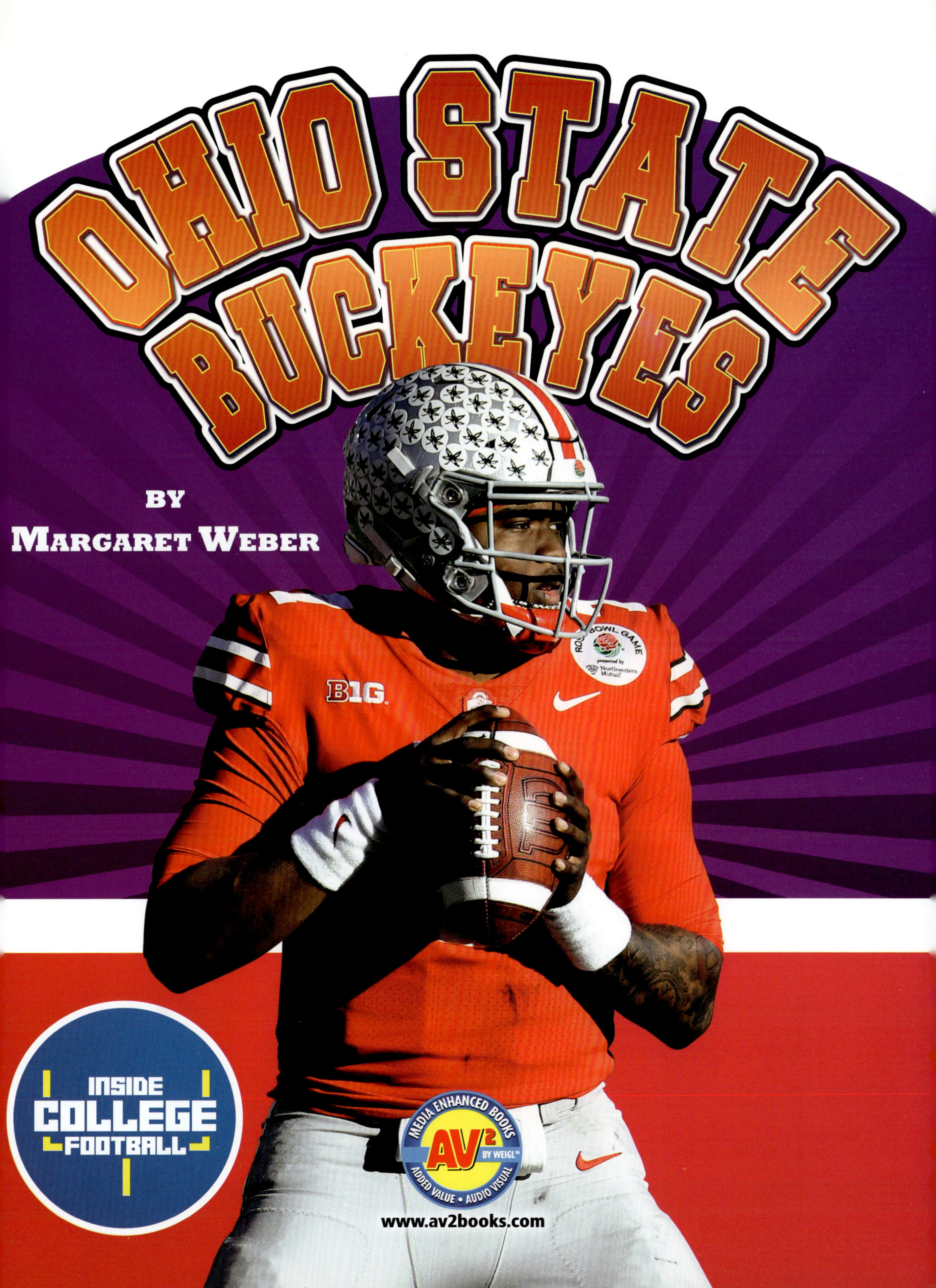
OHIO STATE BUCKEYES
BY
MARGARET WEBER
B1G
INSIDE COLLEGE FOOTBALL
MEDIA ENHANCED BOOKS
AV2 BY WEIGL
ADDED VALUE • AUDIO VISUAL
www.av2books.com

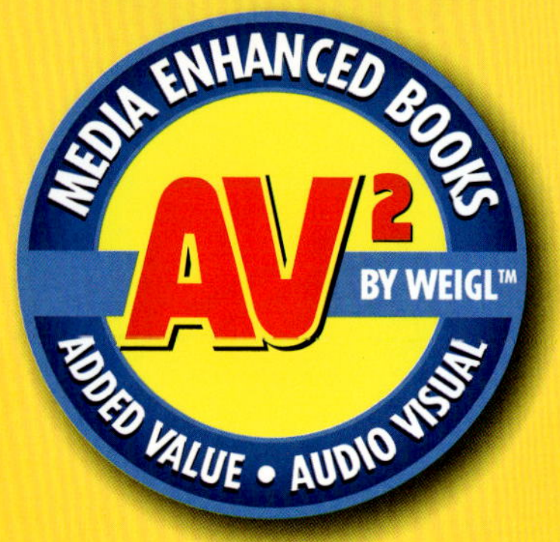

Go to www.av2books.com, and enter this book's unique code.

BOOK CODE

AVV63554

AV² by Weigl brings you media enhanced books that support active learning.

AV² provides enriched content that supplements and complements this book. Weigl's AV² books strive to create inspired learning and engage young minds in a total learning experience.

Your AV² Media Enhanced books come alive with...

Audio
Listen to sections of the book read aloud.

Key Words
Study vocabulary, and complete a matching word activity.

Video
Watch informative video clips.

Quizzes
Test your knowledge.

Embedded Weblinks
Gain additional information for research.

Slideshow
View images and captions, and prepare a presentation.

Try This!
Complete activities and hands-on experiments.

... and much, much more!

Published by AV² by Weigl
350 5th Avenue, 59th Floor
New York, NY 10118
Website: www.av2books.com

Library of Congress Control Number: 2018968204

ISBN 978-1-7911-0068-1 (hardcover)
ISBN 978-1-7911-0069-8 (multi-user eBook)
ISBN 978-1-7911-0070-4 (single-user eBook)

Printed in Guangzhou, China
1 2 3 4 5 6 7 8 9 0 23 22 21 20 19

042019
102318

Project Coordinator: Jared Siemens Designer: Terry Paulhus

Every reasonable effort has been made to trace ownership and to obtain permission to reprint copyright material. The publishers would be pleased to have any errors or omissions brought to their attention so that they may be corrected in subsequent printings.

The publisher acknowledges Alamy, Getty Images, and Newscom as its primary image suppliers for this title.

Ohio State Buckeyes

CONTENTS

Introduction

In 1890, the Ohio Buckeyes stepped onto the football field for the first time. Like many college teams playing in those early years, the game they played looked more like **rugby** than modern-day football. However, with a 20–14 win against Ohio Wesleyan University, a tradition of competitive football was born.

Since 1912, the Buckeyes have been a part of the Big Ten Conference. From this very competitive conference, Ohio State has emerged as one of the best teams in the nation. They have a total of 33 players and coaches admitted to the College Football **Hall of Fame**. These coaches and players have formed the heart of a team that is proud of their history and traditions.

Ohio State defensive end Jonathon Cooper is a key part of the team's defensive line. Cooper recorded his first quarterback sack in Ohio State's win over the University of Maryland in 2016.

Among the many reasons fans flock to watch Ohio State football games are the **rivalries** and game-day traditions that make Ohio State like no other. A study by the *New York Times* even named the Buckeyes as the team with the most fans in the country.

Wide receiver L'Christian Smith was ranked the number-three high school player in the state of Ohio when he was recruited by Ohio State.

OHIO STATE

Stadium Ohio Stadium

Division Big Ten East

Head Coach Ryan Day

Location Columbus, Ohio

National Championships 4

Nicknames Buckeyes

3 Home Stadiums

25 Head Coaches

23 Games Won in a Row from 2014 to 2015

199 All-American Players

History

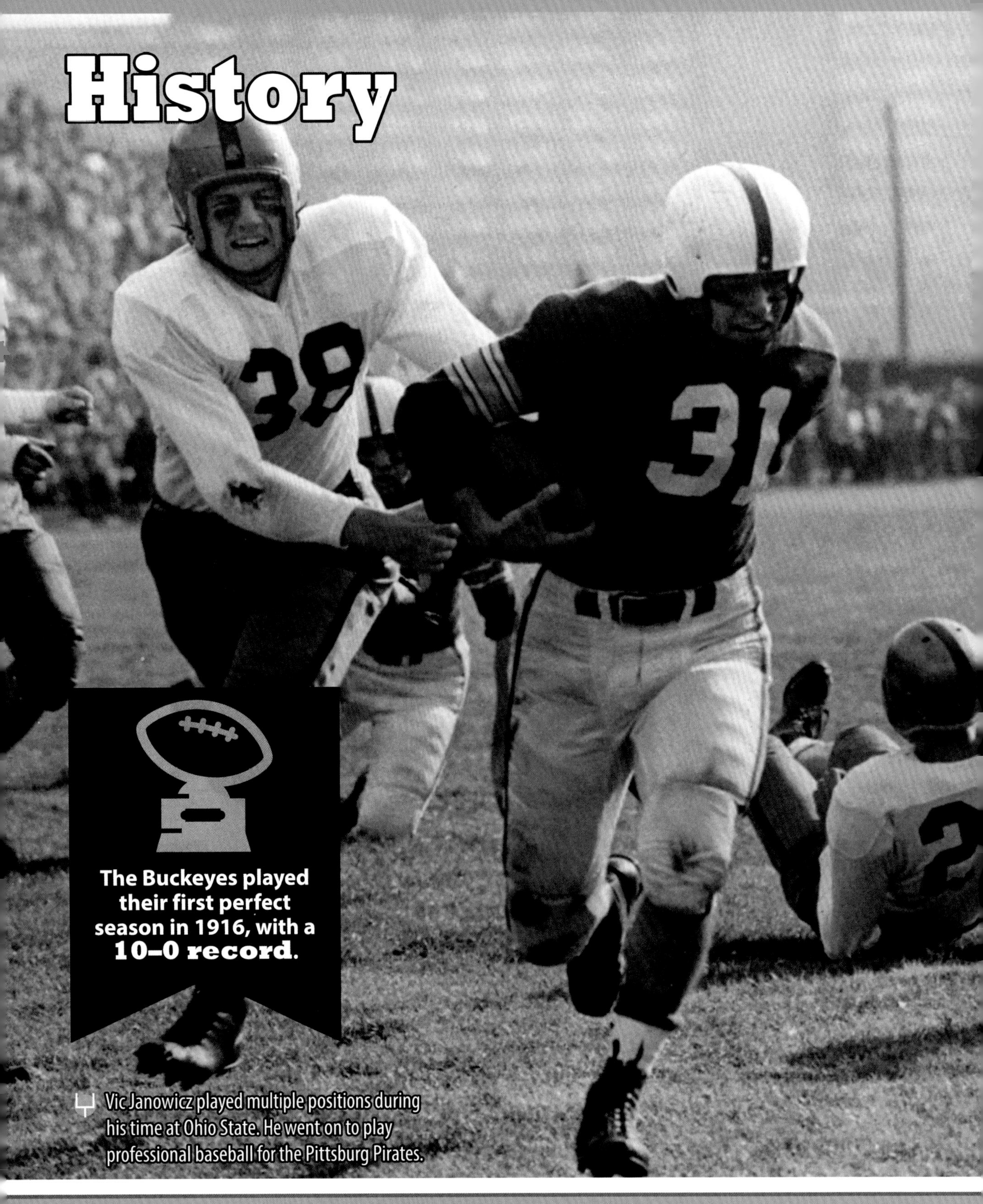

The Buckeyes played their first perfect season in 1916, with a **10–0 record**.

Vic Janowicz played multiple positions during his time at Ohio State. He went on to play professional baseball for the Pittsburg Pirates.

The early years of Buckeyes football were important, but it was not until after **World War II** (1939–1945) that Ohio became a national football force. In the 1950s and 1960s, Ohio State became known as a "football school" as they battled through both successful and challenging years. In 1961, the team was undefeated. This was followed by a few years marked by losses, until they were once again undefeated in 1968. These highs and lows prepared fans for similar years in the early 2000s. In 2014, Ohio State became the first team to win the College Football Playoff National Championship. This solidified the Buckeyes' place in history.

Even before the Buckeyes had successful seasons, fans created traditions to celebrate their favorite team. One of these traditions includes an all-brass marching band that plays during games. The band began playing at games during the 1930s and 1940s.

In addition to the marching band, traditional rivalries are also important. Since 1925, fans have rooted for Ohio State to beat the University of Illinois and take home a carved turtle trophy known as the Illibuck. Any time that the Buckeyes beat their rival, the Michigan Wolverines, all coaches and players are given miniature gold football pants to mark the occasion.

World War II left Ohio State with a roster of mostly freshman and sophomore athletes from 1941 to 1944. Despite the lack of experienced players, Ohio State won two Big Ten championships.

The Stadium

Ohio Stadium is the third-largest college football stadium in the United States.

Construction on Ohio Stadium began in 1921 in Columbus, Ohio. It opened in 1922. Located on the campus of Ohio State University, the stadium quickly became the center of Buckeyes football and a home for both players and fans.

Ohio Stadium is shaped like a long half circle. It is known as the Horseshoe, or just the Shoe. It has seen many improvements, both big and small, throughout the years. As football became more popular, the seating capacity was improved. In 1971, the field was replaced with **AstroTurf**, and in 1990, it was switched back to grass.

The largest renovation took place between 1999 and 2001. Improvements were made to many parts of the stadium, including seating, aisles, lighting, and special club sections. These improvements have only added to the fans' enjoyment of Buckeyes football. Fans of other events have also been able to enjoy Ohio Stadium for events such as concerts and professional soccer. The Horseshoe is a destination for many events outside of football season.

The Rotunda at Ohio Stadium contains three large stained-glass windows that feature a large block "O" and scenes of the Buckeyes in action on the football field.

Where They Play

Welcome to Ohio Stadium. Die-hard fans turn out rain or shine to cheer on their team. For almost two decades, crowds of 100,000 or more have filled the stadium for home football games. A winning team, a top marching band, and many fan traditions make Ohio Stadium one of college football's best.

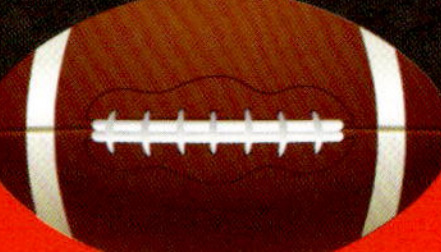

BIG TEN WEST

1. **Northwestern University** *Evanston, Illinois*
2. **Purdue University** *West Lafayette, Indiana*
3. **University of Illinois** *Urbana-Champaign, Illinois*
4. **University of Iowa** *Iowa City, Iowa*
5. **University of Minnesota** *Minneapolis, Minnesota*
6. **University of Nebraska** *Lincoln, Nebraska*
7. **University of Wisconsin** *Madison, Wisconsin*

Arena
Ohio Stadium

Location
Columbus, Ohio

Broke Ground
1921

Completed
1922

Surface
Real Grass

Features
- The scoreboard is 124 feet (38 meters) high
- In 2014, seats were added over the player field entrance
- Listed on the National Register of Historic Places

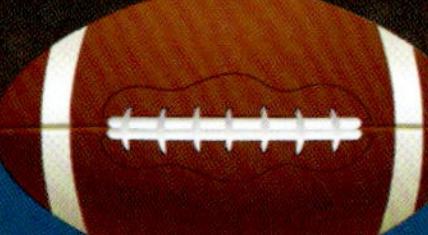

BIG TEN EAST

1. **Indiana University** *Bloomington, Indiana*
2. **Michigan State University** *East Lansing, Michigan*
3. ★ **Ohio State University** *Columbus, Ohio*
4. **Pennsylvania State University** *State College, Pennsylvania*
5. **Rutgers University–New Brunswick** *New Brunswick–Piscataway, New Jersey*
6. **University of Maryland** *College Park, Maryland*
7. **University of Michigan** *Ann Arbor, Michigan*

NORTH DAKOTA
MINNESOTA
WISCONSIN
MICHIGAN
NEW YORK
RHODE ISLAND
CONNECTICUT
NEW JERSEY
SOUTH DAKOTA
IOWA
PENNSYLVANIA
NEBRASKA
ILLINOIS
INDIANA
OHIO
WEST VIRGINIA
VIRGINIA
DELAWARE
MARYLAND
WASHINGTON, D.C.
KANSAS
MISSOURI
KENTUCKY
NORTH CAROLINA
TENNESSEE
SOUTH CAROLINA
OKLAHOMA
ARKANSAS
MISSISSIPPI
ALABAMA
GEORGIA
Atlantic Ocean
TEXAS
LOUISIANA
FLORIDA
Gulf of Mexico
LEGEND
Home Stadium
Big Ten West
Big Ten East
United States
Other Countries
Water
SCALE
0 miles
500 miles
0 kilometers
500 km

The Uniforms

Ohio State's **colors** were chosen by a committee of three students just before graduation in **1878**.

Ohio State's uniforms are made by Nike and feature the Big Ten Conference logo.

The Buckeyes take to the field in their signature colors of scarlet and gray. While some teams stick to the same jerseys and pants in every game, Buckeyes do things a little differently. Fans have come to expect that Ohio State will play in a variety of uniforms. This is one way they honor their long history and celebrate the achievements of Ohio football.

The traditional uniform for the Buckeyes is red with white numbering and letters. However, sometimes the Buckeyes wear special uniforms. For example, in 2013 the Buckeyes **unveiled** a new uniform for their traditional rivalry game against the University of Michigan. In 1950, the two teams met in what is remembered as the "snow bowl." Nine inches of snow fell during the game. More than 50 years later, the Buckeyes wore an all-white uniform in their game against Michigan to commemorate the snowy game. These uniforms bring years of Buckeyes tradition to each game.

Ohio State was one of the first teams to award merit stickers to players for game accomplishments. The Buckeyes have been sporting buckeye leaf merit stickers since 1968.

Student Athletes

In 2018, Ohio State named **seven** players to serve as **captains** of the team.

In 2017, the Buckeyes had the highest average team GPA in eight years. A total of 44 players had a GPA of 3.0 or higher.

Being a college student athlete is hard work. Student athletes have to perform well on the football field and in the classroom. Ohio State student athletes are required to meet a minimum grade point average. Athletes at Ohio State have access to tutors and academic advisors through the Student-Athlete Support Services Office (SASSO). Ohio State and the Big Ten Conference offer several awards and scholarships for student athletes who excel in their studies.

Many student athletes are given athletic scholarships. An athletic scholarship is a financial aid agreement between the athlete and the college or university. Athletes who do not receive an athletic scholarship can be "walk-on" members of the team. This means they are on the team, but without athletic financial aid. Ohio State typically awards the maximum number of football scholarships allowed, which is 85.

Based on the money the team makes from ticket sales, merchandising, and its worth to the university, Ohio State is valued at $1.5 billion. The Buckeyes are one of the most valuable teams in all of college football.

Bowl Games

The first Rose Bowl was played in **1902**, but it did not become an annual event until 1916. Ohio State has played in the Rose Bowl **15** times.

The Buckeyes have been competing in bowl games since 1921, when they played in the Rose Bowl for the first time.

Bowl Games are a unique sports tradition in college football. In the beginning of college football, there was no true **postseason**. Today, a variety of postseason bowl games are played. Bowl games give teams the opportunity to continue striving for recognition and victory after the end of regular play. There are currently 40 bowl games played in various combinations each year. These games are chosen with input from teams, sponsors, and the College Football Playoff Committee. The game matchups are announced in December.

Every bowl game that Ohio State plays in is an important one. However, the games that are remembered best by fans and players are usually those played against rivals. One such rival is the University of Southern California Trojans. The Trojans were victorious over the Buckeyes for a seven-game streak from 1975 to 2009. Ohio State broke the streak in 2017 when they defeated USC 24–7 in the Goodyear Cotton Bowl Classic.

Ohio State and the University of Southern California are fierce rivals. The two teams have met in eight bowl games since 1955, including seven Rose Bowls and a Cotton Bowl.

The Coaches

Alexander Lilley, the **first coach** for the Buckeyes, was known for riding a **pony** to practices.

Ryan Day is Ohio State's 25th head coach. Day was the Buckeyes' offensive coordinator under Urban Meyer from 2017 to 2018, after serving as a quarterback coach in the NFL for two seasons.

The head coach plays an important role in guiding the team. In addition to the head coaches, there is always a staff of additional coaches who focus on certain players or positions. Each head coach has brought talent and opportunity to the team. However, a few standout coaches have led the team to many victories and championship wins.

WOODY HAYES Every Buckeyes fan knows the name of Woody Hayes. His era of Ohio State football built the team that still plays on Woody Hayes Drive. He won 5 national titles, as well as 13 Big Ten championships between 1951 and 1978. He also won four Rose Bowls and three National Coach of the Year Awards during his time with the Buckeyes.

JIM TRESSEL Between 2001 and 2010, the Buckeyes won or shared six Big Ten titles. These titles were the accomplishment of Jim Tressel. This was an important time for Ohio State. Tressel also led the Buckeyes to repeated wins against their rival, the Michigan Wolverines. His 8–1 record against the Wolverines is still celebrated today.

URBAN MEYER Urban Meyer coached the Buckeyes from 2012 to 2018. In his first two seasons with Ohio State, he won 24 of 26 games. Meyer also brought a focus to his players' mental health. He wanted his players to succeed off the field as well as on, so he hosted weekly health seminars for his team during the off-season. Meyer retired from coaching at the end of the 2018 season.

The Mascot

Brutus Buckeye has been inspiring fans to show their devotion to Ohio State for more than 50 years.

Brutus Buckeye appears at Ohio State games to cheer on his team and engage with fans. A buckeye is a nut that is common to the state of Ohio. It is small, shiny, and dark brown in color. The nut is said to bring good luck to anyone who carries one. The team's official name became the Buckeyes in 1950.

Brutus the Buckeye first made his appearance in 1965. He has a buckeye nut as a head, a hat with a large "O" on it, and a scarlet and gray striped shirt. His name is written across the front of his jersey. His number, 00, is on the back, making him easy for fans to spot.

The first Brutus Buckeye costume was a papier-mâché buckeye with holes cut out for a person's legs. Today, Brutus's costume is made up of nine different pieces, including the wristbands and towel.

Legends of the Past

For many players, their time with the Buckeyes is the start of a promising football career. These are some of the best-known football players to play for Ohio State University.

Archie Griffin

Archie Griffin played for the Ohio Buckeyes from 1972 to 1975. During that time, he brought excitement and talent to the team. In Griffin's second game for Ohio State, he rushed 239 yards. He followed this feat by rushing 100 yards in 34 games, setting a NCAA record. Griffin was a two-time **Heisman Memorial Trophy** award winner, and the only player to win twice. He entered the 1976 NFL **draft** as a running back and was drafted in round one. Griffin played in the NFL from 1976 until 1985. His number was retired by Ohio State in 1999.

Position: Running Back
Seasons: 1972–1975 (Ohio State Buckeyes), 1976–1982 (Cincinnati Bengals), 1985 (Jacksonville Bulls)
Born: August 21, 1954, Columbus, Ohio

Michael Thomas

Ohio Buckeyes know how to set records. Michael Thomas, who played with the Buckeyes from 2012 to 2015, is proof of this. He currently holds the NFL record for most receptions. Thomas started with Ohio State as a freshman. In 2014, he led the Buckeyes in receptions. He had a total of 54 receptions and 799 yards gained. That season, he also had nine touchdowns. Thomas also led his team to a 2014 Sugar Bowl victory. He joined the NFL with the New Orleans Saints in 2016 as a starting wide receiver where he continues to play today.

Position: Wide Receiver
Seasons: 2012–2016 (Ohio State Buckeyes), 2016–Present (New Orleans Saints)
Born: March 3, 1993, Los Angeles, California

Eddie George

When Ohio Buckeyes hear the name Eddie George, they might think of number 27. George wore the number at Ohio State, and it was retired when he left the Buckeyes. Although his early seasons were marked by setbacks, he went on to great success. In 1995, he set two Buckeyes records, the first by rushing 1,927 yards. He also scored a record-setting 24 touchdowns. George was awarded the Heisman Trophy in 1995, his senior year at Ohio State. When he left the Buckeyes for the NFL draft, he was second in rushing yards in Ohio State history. Before retiring from his NFL career in 2006, George played for the Tennessee Titans and the Dallas Cowboys.

Position: Running Back
Seasons: 1992–1995 (Ohio State Buckeyes), 1996–2003 (Houston Oilers/Tennessee Titans), 2004 (Dallas Cowboys)
Born: September 24, 1973, Philadelphia, Pennsylvania

Cardale Jones

Cardale Jones is a player that current NFL fans know as a member of the Buffalo Bills and Los Angeles Chargers, but his first home was in Ohio. Born in Cleveland, he joined his home-state Buckeyes in 2012. He was on the third string when injuries to his fellow quarterbacks put him in the game. In 2014, he made his mark by leading his team to a 59–0 victory in his first starting game. He was named **Most Valuable Player (MVP)** of the game. He excelled in passing yards and completions in his senior year. Jones also led his team to a College Football Playoff win. His record as a starting quarterback for the Buckeyes was a perfect 11–0.

Position: Quarterback
Seasons: 2012–2015 (Ohio State Buckeyes), 2016–Present (New Orleans Saints)
Born: September 29, 1992, Cleveland, Ohio

All-Time Records

56

Rushing Touchdowns

Running back Pete Johnson holds the record for all-time rushing touchdowns as a Buckeye, with a total of 56 between 1973 and 1976.

30

Points Scored by a Single Player in a Single Game

In 2013, running back Carlos Hyde scored 30 points against Illinois, setting the all-time Buckeyes record.

9,434

Career Passing Yards

Former Ohio State quarterback J.T. Barrett holds the Buckeyes' record for the most passing yards of all time. Barrett passed for 9,434 yards and completed 769 out of 1,211 attempted passes.

110,045

Fans in Attendance

The all-time record for fan attendance at a Buckeyes game was set in 2016, when 110,045 fans attended a game against Michigan State.

72

Most Field Goals Made

Kicker Mike Nugent holds the record for most field goals made at Ohio State, with 72 field goals.

Timeline

Throughout the team's history, the Ohio State Buckeyes have had many memorable events that have become defining moments for the team and its fans.

The Buckeyes play their first season in 1890.

1900 1920 1940 1960

1899
The Ohio State Buckeyes win a championship for the first time. This is an important turning point in the Buckeyes' history. This season is the first in a 23-year winning streak.

1951
Renowned coach Woody Hayes takes over. He is hired with a unanimous vote from the Board of Trustees. His arrival marks an important era of Buckeyes football.

1954
The Ohio State Buckeyes celebrate a perfect 10–0 season. It is capped off with an amazing 20–7 win over Southern California in a muddy Rose Bowl game.

1968
Coach Hayes begins rewarding his players with decals in recognition of good plays. These decals become a recognizable presence on the field.

The Future

The Buckeyes are looking forward to successful seasons in the future. Although Coach Meyer is retiring, he is leaving the Buckeyes in the capable hands of Coach Day, who plans to maintain Ohio State's high standards. They are poised to take even more championships and to continue as one of the best football programs in the country.

1969

The Ohio State Buckeyes end a 22-game winning streak with a loss to the Michigan Wolverines. This game sets off a decade known as the Border War, in which Ohio and Michigan battle for championships and deepen their rivalry.

2016

The Buckeyes have the fewest returning starters, but still win 11 games total, suggesting a bright future awaits the team.

1980 | 2000 | 2020

1995

This is the third year that Buckeyes players take home big awards, including the Heisman Trophy won by Eddie George.

In 2006, the rivalry between Michigan and Ohio is at an all time high. The teams are both undefeated and top the college rankings in the first and second slots. The 2006 game is nicknamed "the Game of the Century." The Ohio Buckeyes are victorious, winning 42–39.

1972

Archie Griffin, considered one of the greatest Buckeyes of all time, begins his record-setting career.

Write a Biography

Life Story

A person's life story can be the subject of a book. This kind of book is called a biography. Biographies often describe the lives of people who have achieved great success. These people may be alive today, or they may have lived many years ago. Reading a biography can help you learn more about a great person.

Get the Facts

Use this book, and research in the library and on the internet, to find out more about your favorite player. Learn as much about him as you can. What position does he play? What are his statistics in important categories? Has he set any records? Also, be sure to write down key events in the person's life. What was his childhood like? What has he accomplished off the field? Is there anything else that makes this person special or unusual?

Use the Concept Web

A concept web is a useful research tool. Read the questions in the concept web on the following page. Answer the questions in your notebook. Your answers will help you write a biography.

Concept Web

Adulthood
- Where does this individual currently reside?
- Does he have a family?

Your Opinion
- What did you learn from the books you read in your research?
- Would you suggest these books to others?
- Was anything missing from these books?

Childhood
- Where and when was this person born?
- Describe his parents, siblings, and friends.
- Did he grow up in unusual circumstances?

Accomplishments off the Field
- What is this person's life's work?
- Has he received awards or recognition for accomplishments?
- How have this person's accomplishments served others?

Write a Biography

Help and Obstacles
- Did this individual have a positive attitude?
- Did he receive help from others?
- Did this person have a mentor?
- Did this person face any hardships?
- If so, how were the hardships overcome?

Accomplishments on the Field
- What records does this person hold?
- What key games and plays have defined his career?
- What are his stats in categories important to his position?

Work and Preparation
- What was this person's education?
- What was his work experience?
- How does this person work?
- What is the process he uses?

Trivia Time

Take this quiz to test your knowledge of the Ohio State Buckeyes. The answers are printed upside down under each question.

1 What is the name of the Ohio State mascot?

A. Brutus Buckeye

2 In what year did the Buckeyes begin playing football?

A. 1890

3 When was Ohio Stadium completed?

A. 1922

4 What team did Ohio State play against in "the Game of the Century"?

A. Michigan

5 In what year was the "snow bowl" played?

A. 1950

6 When did Ohio end the University of Southern California's bowl game winning streak?

A. 2017

7 What are the team colors for the Ohio Buckeyes?

A. Scarlet and gray

8 What position does Cardale Jones play?

A. Quarterback

9 Who holds the Ohio State record for all-time rushing touchdowns?

A. Pete Johnson

10 How many games did Ohio State win in a row between 2014 and 2015?

A. 23

Key Words

AstroTurf: grass-like surface that is made from rubber and plastics

draft: an annual event where the NFL chooses college football players to be new team members

Hall of Fame: a group of persons judged to be outstanding in a particular sport

Heisman Memorial Trophy: an annual award given to the college football player who best demonstrates excellence and hard work

Most Valuable Player (MVP): the player judged to be most valuable to his team's success

postseason: a sporting event that takes place after the end of the regular season

rivalries: competitions between different groups or individuals toward the same objective or goal

rugby: a team game played with an oval ball that can be kicked, carried, or passed

unveiled: to show something in public for the first time

World War II: a war from 1939 to 1945 between seven countries

Index

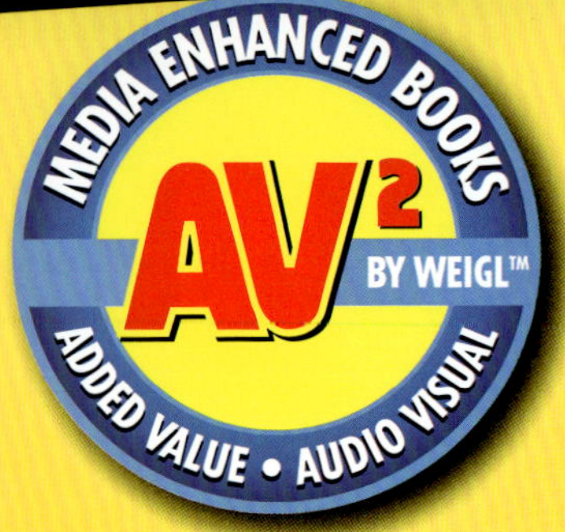

Log on to www.av2books.com

AV² by Weigl brings you media enhanced books that support active learning. Go to www.av2books.com, and enter the special code found on page 2 of this book. You will gain access to enriched and enhanced content that supplements and complements this book. Content includes video, audio, weblinks, quizzes, a slideshow, and activities.

AV² Online Navigation

Audio
Listen to sections of the book read aloud.

Book Pages
AV² pages directly correspond to pages in the book.

Video
Watch informative video clips.

Embedded Weblinks
Gain additional information for research.

Key Words
Study vocabulary, and complete a matching word activity.

Try This!
Complete activities and hands-on experiments.

Quizzes
Test your knowledge.

Slideshow
View images and captions, and prepare a presentation.

AV² was built to bridge the gap between print and digital. We encourage you to tell us what you like and what you want to see in the future.

Sign up to be an AV² Ambassador at www.av2books.com/ambassador.

Due to the dynamic nature of the internet, some of the URLs and activities provided as part of AV² by Weigl may have changed or ceased to exist. AV² by Weigl accepts no responsibility for any such changes. All media enhanced books are regularly monitored to update addresses and sites in a timely manner. Contact AV² by Weigl at 1-866-649-3445 or av2books@weigl.com with any questions, comments, or feedback.